HOW TO WRITE
AUDIO AND
VIDEO SCRIPTS

ELT Teacher 2 Writer

John Hughes

TRAINING COURSE FOR ELT WRITERS

How To Write Audio And Video Scripts
By John Hughes
This edition © 2019 ELT Teacher 2 Writer
www.eltteacher2writer.co.uk

The author would like to thank the following people for giving their time freely and contributing ideas to the book: Mari Tudor Jones (MTJ Media), Diarmuid Carter (Digeo Productions), James Magrane (Oxford University Press), James Tomalin (Oxford Digital Media), Martyn Gretton (Cambridge Media Solutions) and Tom Dick & Debbie Video Production.

The author and publishers would like to thank the following for permission to reproduce their material: National Geographic Learning, Oxford University Press.

Contents

About The Author

Interviewer: What's your name?
Me: John Hughes.
Interviewer: Where are you from?
Me: England. Now I live near Oxford but I've taught students and trained teachers in many other countries.
Interviewer: How did you get into ELT?
Me: I was studying performances of Shakespeare for an MA in central and Eastern Europe and while I was in Poland a university approached me about doing some lecturing on a drama course. They also needed Business English teachers so I started teaching those. I liked teaching Business English straight away because business communication skills are so much about language with performance.

Interviewer: So, does your interest in scripts come from your interest in drama?

Me: To some extent. I've studied radio drama and I also worked with TV companies including the satirical *Spitting Image* in the late 80s so I suppose I've spent a number of years listening to scripts and thinking about the key ingredients.

Interviewer: When did you start writing materials for ELT?

Me: As soon as I started teaching in 1992. In particular, I had a lot of Business English and English for Specific Purposes courses, so students would give me texts related to their jobs and I'd turn them into classroom materials.

Interviewer: You published your first ELT book in 2005. How many books have you written since then?

Me: I don't know exactly because I've worked on all sorts of projects either as an author or co-author. For example, I'm a co-author on the series *Business Result* (OUP) and *Life* (National Geographic Learning) and I've also written numerous components such as teacher's books and workbooks for other courses. So, I've either written or co-authored well over 40 titles and at least two thirds of those have either an audio or video component. Increasingly, I'm writing online materials which also need scripts, especially for video.

Interviewer: Is that why you've written this book? Because materials writers need to write more and more scripts?

Me: Yes, although writing scripts has always been important in ELT; even before recording technology was invented, the earliest examples of textbooks include scripted dialogues on the page. It's a skill that all materials writers need but I also know lots of teachers who like writing their own audio scripts or making videos for their lessons so, hopefully this book will help them to develop that skill.

Interviewer: I'm sure it will. Thanks for talking to me John. Where can people find out more information about your books?
Me: At www.johnhugheselt.com

Aims And Introductory Task

The basic aims of this book about writing audio and video scripts are to:

1   provide an overview of the theoretical and practical issues involved in writing audio and video scripts for ELT materials.

2   provide you with a framework which can guide you in the writing of scripts for audio and video components in ELT materials.

3   provide practical suggestions on writing scripts for audio and video and to provide a wide range of models.

4   encourage you to think critically about script writing for audio and video.

Note
This book focuses primarily on materials for adult and secondary school learners.

Task 1

Before you start reading this book, make notes about your answers to this introductory task. Keep the notes somewhere safe so you can refer back to them later.

1. To write audio and video scripts, materials writers need a number of skills and abilities. Look at the following list and rank these abilities in order of importance from 1 to 6 (1 = most important, 6 = least important):

- ability to grade the language to the correct level
- ability to target language to include in an audio script
- ability to write scripts that sound authentic
- ability to listen to real speech and identify features of discourse
- ability to create credible dramatic narratives and characters
- ability to format audio and video scripts using scriptwriting conventions

2. Can you think of any other skills or abilities a writer of audio and video might need to develop for ELT materials writing?

3. Which of the above abilities do you feel you already possess to some extent? Which will you need to work on and develop while you read?

1. A Short History Of Writing Scripts For ELT Materials

Writing scripts for language learning materials is one part of what the modern ELT writer is required to do. Scripts often take the form of monologues or dialogues which are then recorded and which make up part of a coursebook package or appear in the form of online self-study materials. Increasingly, ELT writers are also writing scripts for video materials. Whether it's for audio or video, for a CD or an MP3 file, for a DVD or a video on YouTube, scripts are often something we tend to associate with the modern world of ELT. However, writing scripts (and especially dialogues) is not *just* a feature of modern ELT materials. In fact, they appear in some of the very earliest materials written for language learners. This section provides a brief overview of how scripts have evolved in materials writing over the last five centuries and illustrates the reasons why it's such an important – and influential – aspect of materials writing.

EARLY SCRIPTS IN LANGUAGE LEARNING MATERIALS

In *A History of English Language Teaching*, Howatt and Widdowson provide examples of language learning materials taken from early handbooks written for learners of English. Many of the earliest extracts take the form of scripted dialogues on the page; for example, the following dialogue is set at a dining table and appeared in a handbook published in 1554 called *A Very Profitable Book*. Written specifically for Spanish learners of English, the English version and the Spanish translation would have originally been placed side-by-side on the page:

Hermes: John, I pray God send ye a good day.
John: And I, Hermes, wish unto you a prosperous day.
Hermes: How do you?
John: Ask you how I do? I fare well, thanks be to God,
and will be glad to do you pleasure. I say, Hermes, how
go matters forward?
Hermes: Verily I fare well.

Quoted in Howatt, A.P.R & Widdowson, H.G. (2004) *A History of English Language Teaching* Oxford, p15

Although the English is old, the actual context and rationale behind this text feels quite contemporary; after all, it provides students with the language for meeting people for the first time and making small talk so if updated it wouldn't feel out of place in any modern business English coursebook. Another book from the same century contains nothing but scripted dialogues. Published in 1586 for French-speaking refugees entering England, *Familiar Dialogues* is a collection of dialogues which 'have a domestic setting with a strong emphasis on shopping … The book ends with some useful travel phrases.' (pp22–3)

What's interesting about many of these early examples of scripted ELT materials is how they focus on the learners' needs and provide functional and useful phrases in a context; much in the same way that the modern ELT writers try to do today; the only difference being that they were not recorded but probably read aloud by the teacher and the students had to memorise the dialogues by heart.

Later textbooks also include scripted dialogues which weren't necessarily functional but were used in a question-and-answer approach in order to explain points of grammar or other areas of language. This example of such a dialogue is from a Russian textbook published in 1795 (p71):

> *Teacher:* When is g pronounced?
> *Pupil:* G is pronounced soft when it precedes e, i, and y, for example, gender, ginger, gipsy.
> *Teacher:* Are there exceptions?
> *Pupil:* The letter g is pronounced hard before e and i in the following words: gelderland, gibbons, gilman ...

Howatt and Widdowson also report on another book published only two years later in 1797 designed to aid pronunciation by listing sets of words (including nonsense syllables) for the student to practise such as *lip, nip, pip, rip, sip.* This kind of listing of words for students to pronounce is not greatly different from what modern ELT writers do when they script simple 'listen and repeat' type pronunciation exercises for low-level materials.

The 19th century is generally associated with the period of the Grammar-Translation Method[1] and the growth in languages as a formal school subject. Typically, we think of rows of pupils reading and translating long written texts on the page and therefore little room for students learning to speak with the use of scripted conversations. Whilst there are in fact examples of materials from the 1800s which include phrases and question-and-answer dialogues in a semi-scripted format, the end of the 19th century and

---

[1] **Grammar-Translation**
A method of teaching based on the way in which Latin was once taught. Grammar is regarded as being at the centre of language teaching and is formally presented to the students and then tested by having students translate sentences either into their own language or from their own language into English. This method of teaching was highly influential on the language classroom into the early and middle part of the 20th century.

the rise of the Direct Method and the Natural Method[2] is more significant in terms of script writing.

Both methods placed the emphasis on asking the student genuine questions that require a real answer; for example *What's the time?* The coursebook writer and school owner Maximilian Berlitz is probably the most famous name associated with these movements. While he didn't invent the Direct Method, he introduced it to many language learners via his many schools and textbooks. His famous *First Book* (first published in 1906 with many new editions printed in later years) contains a variety of scripts which a teacher and student would have read aloud in class. Many of these scripts are formulaic and artificial language drill exercises which introduce a grammar item, like this one in the ninth lesson of the book:

> *Me, him, her, us, them*
> *I give you a book. What do I do?*
> *Give me a pencil. What do you do?*
> *I give a box to Mr White. What do I give (to) Mr*
> *White? You give him a box.*

M.D. Berlitz *First Book* (333rd Edition 1924), p27

In the second half of the book, there is a section of reading passages which often take the form of mini-conversations. Unlike the language drills earlier in the book, these scripted

---

[2] **Direct Method / Natural Method**
The Direct and Natural Methods were two approaches that emerged in the late 19th century in reaction to Grammar Translation (see footnote 1). They emphasised use of the first language only in order to reflect the way a first language is learned 'naturally'. Learners were exposed to the spoken form before the written form so teachers often followed scripted dialogues with students.

conversations have a context. Here is the opening extract aimed at introducing students to the language of travel:

The arrival

A. – We shall soon be at the station. We had better roll up our rugs and get our valises down.
B. – At what hotel shall we stop?
A. – We can stop at Charing Cross, because it is so centrally located, not expensive, and it will be very convenient when we leave for Paris, as it is connected with the station.
B. – The train is stopping. What an immense station! Shall I call the porter?
A. – If you please.
B. – Here, porter! Take these two bags to a cab. You can carry the rugs also.
Porter – Here is the cab, Sir. Have you anything besides your hand-luggage?

M.D. Berlitz *First Book* (333rd Edition 1924), p67

By writing materials like this, Berlitz didn't need to employ highly trained teachers with an understanding of the student's first language (as had been the case with grammar-translation) but, instead, Berlitz teachers simply needed to follow a script. This conversational approach or 'direct method' proved especially popular with the growing number of students who needed English (or other languages) for business and travel purposes in the early part of the 20th century.

THE INTRODUCTION OF RECORDING TECHNOLOGY IN THE CLASSROOM

About 20 years before Berlitz's first publication, Thomas Edison had invented the phonograph which could record human speech. Years later, as recording technology evolved, it eventually became a central feature of the language classroom but by the 50s and 60s the Direct Method had 'metamorphosed into audiolingualism[3]'. (Thornbury, S. (2006) *An A–Z of ELT* Macmillan Education, p66). Essentially, the Audiolingual method stressed the value of having students listen to and repeat sentences in a continuous drill pattern.

The natural manifestation of audiolingualism was the language laboratory. By the 1970s classes of students might be found in rooms of cubicles, each with a set of headphones. The teacher's role was to play a variety of recordings and – in theory – monitor each student's individual progress. Many language laboratory sessions began with the student listening to a scripted passage and completing comprehension tasks. As the class progressed however, a student would be expected to listen and respond.

In the passage below, the student has listened to model versions of questions and sentences based on a series of small pictures of grocery items bought while shopping. Now it his/her chance to play an active role in the scripted dialogue. Note that the student would have heard the

---

[3] **Audiolingualism (also Audiolingual Method)**
Audiolingualism was based on the belief that language learning was about habit formation. Learners listened to and repeated dialogues in the form of a drill. As recording technology developed, the idea of classrooms as language laboratories emerged with rows of learners wearing headphones and the teacher controlling what each student was listening to.

exercise number and rubric given at the beginning – a mechanical but nonetheless important aspect for this type of ELT script writing:

> *Exercise 3. Now play the part of a customer. Look at picture 1. Listen.*
> **Voice:** *Good morning. Can I help you?*
> **Student:** *I'd like five oranges. How much is that?*
>
> *Look at picture 2.*
> **Voice:** *Good morning. Can I help you?*
> **Student:** *I'd like half a dozen eggs. How much is that?*
>
> *Look at picture 3.*
> **Voice:** *Good morning. Can I help you?*
> **Student:** *I'd like two loaves of bread. How much is that?*

Dakin, J. (1973) *The language laboratory and language learning* Longman, p124

Despite criticism for its lack of authenticity and drilling, we can still see the influence of this kind of audiolingual scripting on modern language learning materials, especially those sold for self-study such as 'listen-and-learn-a-language-in-the-car' type audio recordings or teach-yourself computer-based programmes. In other words, it is a type of script writing that many modern ELT writers still write from time to time.

WRITING SCRIPTS FOR COMMUNICATIVE LANGUAGE TEACHING (CLT) MATERIALS

Towards the late 70s, there was a growing demand for materials to include audio recordings which, if they weren't entirely authentic, at least reflected the need for learners to achieve communicative competence. As we have already seen, writing scripts with model dialogues was nothing new but there was a renewed emphasis in communicative language teaching on authenticity[4] and functional/situational[5] type language. However, what made materials around this time distinct from the past was that coursebooks started to focus on skills development; in other words, the contents page of a book might include a column on developing the skills of reading, writing, speaking and – most relevantly – listening. So the tape cassettes which were sold with these books not only included dialogues and mini-conversations but also longer spoken texts which were scripted to develop listening sub-skills in some way. Many of these listening scripts were written in the style of news broadcasts or journalistic interviews but graded to the target level. Such types of listening script still appear in coursebooks to this day, like this extract from a book preparing students for the Cambridge Assessment English B2 First (FCE):

---

[4] **authenticity**

In recent years, ELT materials have put an emphasis on the use of authentic texts in the classroom. For example, using articles from real newspapers or recordings from TV documentaries. In contrast, coursebooks have been criticised for their inauthenticity with their gapfill exercises and drills. Nowadays, most teachers and writers assume that a mixture of authenticity and inauthenticity is desirable. As a result, many published texts and scripts tend to be 'realistic' rather than '100% authentic'.

[5] **functional-situational**

This refers to the approach in a syllabus or materials to present language as functions and/or in a situation. For example, you might have the function of 'asking for information about a product' and the situation is 'at the shop'. This way of organising language is typically used in tourist phrasebooks and materials that help learners prepare for using English in specific contexts (e.g. travelling abroad).

Listening 13.1

Newsreader: *Have you heard about a new report on education which says these are the worst results in over 20 years and one ex-headmaster said the situation is appalling? That's the verdict on the spelling ability of school children in Great Britain after the results of last year's national tests were released. The report reveals that pupils who were tested, aged 11 and 14, made more spelling errors than they did four years ago ...*

Extract from Hughes, J & Naunton, J. *Spotlight on FCE* (2009) National Geographic Learning

THE EMERGENCE OF VIDEO

In the 1980s, a newer technology was starting to have an impact on ELT publishing and materials writing. The growing accessibility of VHS video meant that language schools might have at least one video player and TV in their school. The 'video lesson' proved a popular draw for students and some language schools even used it as a unique selling feature of their courses. In response, publishers brought out whole courses based around learning from a video, or producing video as an add-on to a coursebook. The author Ben Goldstein in his article *A History of ELT Video* (*teachingenglish.org.uk/article/ben-goldstein-a-history-video-elt*) comments on one such early attempt to teach English via video:

'*Follow Me*, the BBC video crash course from the late 70s, is a revealing way to see how video was used in the beginning. The series commonly showed functional language contexts with heavily scripted and rather unnatural dialogue. The purpose of the video was language focus. Learners would watch the sketches and use them as a model for their own output. In fact, the video was exploited no differently to audio.'

That the exploitation of ELT video is often no different to audio is a criticism often levelled at ELT materials and it's an issue to which we'll return again later in this book. In fairness to a series like *Follow Me*, while many of its episodes (some of which you can still watch on *YouTube* today) did cover predictable functional language, its scripts did attempt to add drama and intrigue, and many of the locations and settings were ambitious.

By the 90s, other ELT video courses such as the *Grapevine* (OUP) videos had become very popular but video had a long way to go before it became commonplace in every classroom and most ELT script writing remained confined to writing for audio, not video. In an interview with the co-author of the successful *Grapevine* videos and 12 other video courses, Vicki Hollett asks Peter Viney to look back at his period of video and script writing and he remarks that, 'For years I'd tell [teachers] that in the future teachers would use video in every single lesson and I was completely wrong. It didn't happen.' You can watch an extract from Vicki Hollett's video interview at *youtube.com/watch?v=JMBpDmH8W2s*.

In the period that Viney is describing, video tapes were relatively expensive and the cost of the equipment to play it on was a significant amount for the average language school, which may explain why video remained the 'fun' lesson and not a common feature of any lesson. However, the arrival of *YouTube* in 2005 and the increase of digital projectors or IWBs in classroom suddenly made it more possible that teachers might use video in every lesson.

Reflecting the growth in video usage in the classroom, more and more ELT writers are now writing video scripts;

some of these still have a functional language focus as in the past but increasingly ELT video script writing is more varied. For example, this script is an extract from a video about a real school which trains butlers. It contains documentary footage of the trainee butlers talking and narration that has been scripted for the level of the learners who will watch the video. The job of the script writer here is to script the narration and to mix it in with the authentic language of the people in the video. The script also contains reference to what we can see on screen.

> **Narrator**: *Long ago, England was a land of country houses, palaces, gardens and afternoon tea. Every real gentleman had servants, especially a butler. Just 70 years ago, there were tens of thousands of butlers in England. Now there are only a few. So where does one find a good butler nowadays? The Ivor Spencer International School for Butler Administration, of course.*
>
> **Butler 1:** *Good evening, sir. My name's Michael. I'm your butler.*
>
> **Butler 2:** *My name is José.*
>
> **Butler 3:** *I'm your butler.*
>
> **Butler 4:** *Can I bring you some refreshments, sir?*
>
> **Butler 3:** *I'm your butler.*
>
> **Butler 5:** *Good evening, sir.*
>
> **Narrator:** *It's the first day of class and the students are learning how to introduce themselves to their 'gentlemen' or 'lady'. A proper butler must also learn how to carry himself correctly.*

Extract from *Butler School*, National Geographic Learning

THE PRESENT DAY

So, in this short history, we've seen the origins of script writing for ELT materials and how it has evolved (or not at times). Nowadays, student books, workbooks and online materials still require audio scripts. In addition, the dramatic rise in video over the last decade and the fact that it is relatively cheap to produce means that ELT courses will want more and more video scripts. From drills to dialogues, dramas to documentaries, the aim of this book is to help you write them.

Task 2

Choose a mainstream coursebook or online course that you are currently using or are familiar with. Consider the following questions about the audio and/or video scripts of the course in relation to the brief history you have just read:

1. Can you see any similarities between the approach to some of the scripts in the early course materials and the scripts in the course you are looking at? For example, how much does it use dialogues? Listen-and-repeat drills? Videos with drama or documentary?

2. How much difference is there between the ELT scripts in the modern course and those from the past?

3. What do you think the earlier attempts of materials writers and their scripts can tell us about how we should approach scripts for language teaching nowadays?

2. How To Write Audio Scripts

TYPES OF AUDIO SCRIPTS

Task 3

1. Make a list of all the different types of things you have listened to in the last few days; e.g. the news, a quiz show.

2. Compare your list with the types of listening scripts in published materials; e.g. in a coursebook. How similar or different are the types of listening in real life and in the book?

The types of audio script you might be required to write either for your own lessons or for publishers can be quite varied. Here's a list of listening text types that can appear on the Cambridge Assessment English B2 First (FCE) Listening paper 3. It's a good reflection of the types of listening texts that often appear in many ELT materials.

Monologues: answerphone messages, radio documentaries and features, news, public announcements, stories and anecdotes, talks

Interacting speakers: conversations, interviews, discussions, radio plays

Cambridge English First *Handbook For Teachers* 2015

THE PURPOSE OF THE AUDIO

Before you start writing your own audio script, you obviously need to understand how it will be used in the teaching material; in other words, what is the language aim?

Most commonly, ELT audio scripts are written for the following reasons:

1   To develop listening skills (e.g. listening for gist, listening for detail)

2   To practise an aspect of pronunciation (e.g. listening for the stressed syllable of a word)

3   To introduce an item of grammar and/or of vocabulary (e.g. the target language is contextualised in the listening and given higher frequency than you might hear in an authentic script)

4   To introduce useful expressions for a real situation (e.g. asking for directions in the street)

Task 4

Read four audio scripts taken from a pre-intermediate level general English coursebook. For each script, decide what the primary purpose of the script is. For example, do you think it is used to develop listening skills in general or is it to introduce a language item or practise an aspect of pronunciation? Also try to imagine what type of rubric and exercise would accompany the script in the main part of the book; for example, would the student be asked to listen and fill gaps, answer comprehension questions, or listen and repeat the words or sentences?

Audio script 1

Nick Veasey takes photographs of ordinary people, places and objects but no one could describe the final photographs as ordinary. In fact, they are very creative. Nick uses X-ray photography and, as a result, you see inside the object. The final images are often beautiful, strange or surprising. Working with X-rays can be dangerous because of the radiation. So safety always comes first for Nick. His well-equipped studio is a large black building. It has thick concrete walls to stop the radiation. Inside he has different X-ray machines for different sizes and types of images. But not everything he photographs will fit in the studio so sometimes he has to travel to them. For example, he has photographed an aeroplane, a bus and an office building with people working inside. These kinds of projects take many days and many different X-rays. Then, he takes the best image back to his studio and spends a lot of his working day improving the image on his computer until it is ready for an exhibition. You can see his photos in galleries all over the world and many companies also use his images in their advertisements.

Audio script 2
J = Javier, T = Ticket office clerk
J: A return ticket to the airport, please.
T: OK. The next train goes in five minutes.
J: Right. That one, please.
T: First or second class?
J: Second.
T: OK. That's £14.50.
J: Wow! Can I pay by cheque?
T: Sorry. Cash or credit card.
J: Oh no … Oh, one moment. Maybe I have enough left.
T: OK. Here you are.
J: Which platform is it?
T: Err, platform six.

Audio script 3

1. Single or return?	4. Bus or train?
2. Window or aisle?	5. North or south?
3. Credit card or cash?	6. First or second?

Audio script 4

I = Interviewer, E = Engineer

I: How long have you worked for your company?

E: For 25 years. Since I left college.

I: So, when did you study engineering?

E: I started college when I was 19 and I qualified as an engineer about four years later.

I: And have you always lived in Pennsylvania?

E: No. I've lived in lots of different places. In the energy business, you live where the work is.

I: So when did you move here?

E: In 2007. Just after they found the gas here.

I: So, how many different places have you lived in, do you think?

E: I'd say about 15, maybe 16 places.

I: Have you ever lived abroad?

E: Yes, but only for about three months.

I: And how does Pennsylvania compare with other places? Has it been easy living here?

E: Yes, it has, overall.

I: Have the local people been friendly?

E: Yes, they have. Well, most people anyway.

You can read a commentary on this task on page 76.

Extracts from Dummett, Hughes, Stephenson *Life Pre-Intermediate* (2013) National Geographic Learning

Task 5

Look at six language items taken from the contents page of a general English coursebook. In each case, think of an audio text type which naturally incorporates the target language. For example, item 1 would lend itself to a presentation about how something technical works or a dialogue between two people in an office in which one person asks the other for help with a piece of equipment.

1. Verbs for giving instructions (e.g. *press*, *turn*, etc.) with sequencing language (e.g. *First of all*, *after that*, etc.)
2. The first and second conditional
3. A lexical set of film genres (e.g. *sci-fi*, *romantic comedy*, etc.)
4. Collocations with the verbs *make* and *do*.
5. The pronunciation feature of contrastive stress.
6. Useful phrases for asking for directions.

You can read a commentary on this task on page 77.

BALANCING REAL SPEECH WITH GRADED SPEECH

As we have seen, scripted audio is often written so that it presents target language in context as well as providing listening practice. However, this kind of scripted audio recorded for use in coursebooks and student materials is sometimes criticised.

Task 6

Think about whether you have ever heard teachers and/or students complain about the recorded audio in course materials? What kinds of comments have they made?

One major complaint is that the listenings in the course materials are not authentic enough and don't prepare students for listening to real speech. Such a criticism is to miss the point about graded, scripted audio. It is written to the current level of the students or slightly above their level in order to improve their English. If the purpose of the audio were simply to reproduce authentic speech or listenings, then a teacher could simply play authentic recordings; however, the reality is that many students at B2 level and below would not be able to understand them.

However, there is an important issue here that part of our job as audio script writers is to try and include some elements of real speech in order to help students prepare for the real world. In this way, we need to try and find a balance. For example, imagine a writer has produced this listening script for a unit in an A2 coursebook which aims to teach students the language for finding somewhere to eat:

> **Tourist:** *Is there a good place to eat near here?*
> **Local:** *Yes, there is. There's an Italian restaurant on the corner. It serves delicious pasta. Go straight down the street and it's in front of you.*
> **Tourist:** *I prefer Indian food. Are there any Indian restaurants near here?*
> **Local:** *Yes, there are two. My favourite is on Gower Street. Go straight ahead, take the first right and it's on your left.*

Extract from *Life Elementary Video*, *Unit 3*, National Geographic Learning

The script is at the right level and it introduces some useful vocabulary and expressions for giving directions. You can probably picture the type of exercise that might go with it; perhaps a simple gapfill exercise where you listen and write in some key missing words or phrases, or a map where you have to label with the names of the restaurants. In fact, overall, it's very typical of what you might find in many low-level course materials.

Now compare it to two more conversations which were recorded with real people in a street in Oxford. The interviewer walked up to them and asked them to talk about places to eat that they'd recommend in the local area. So, these two scripts are 100% authentic and illustrate some key features of real speech:

> ***Speaker 1:*** *Yeah, there are some places, I mean there are some choices which is Italian, Turkish, Greek and, err, burger, pizza places.*
> ***Speaker 2:*** *There are several good places to eat round here. It's a good road for it. There's the Greek place err just there, err there's the Italian over the road, there is the American style Atomic Burgers down there who also have a pizzeria at the other end.*

Extract from *Life Elementary Video*, National Geographic Learning

These two short authentic scripts illustrate some key features of real speech which are often omitted from scripted audio. They are as follows:

False starts and repetition
Speaker 1 makes a false start in his response when he says *there are some places, I mean there are some choices ...*

He begins speaking and then decides to start again. He also repeats the words, *There are ... there* are. This kind of feature is common in everyday speech but rarely reproduced in graded scripts.

Error

Both non-native and native speakers alike make 'errors' in natural speech. In the examples above, the verb (*to be*) doesn't agree with the subject in Speaker 1's opening sentence so he uses *is* instead of *are*:

> *... there are some choices which is Italian, Turkish, Greek and, err, Burger, Pizza places.*

Fillers and filled pauses

Both speakers use the most common filler *err* while they think for the next word. Speaker 1 also uses the filler *I mean*.

Contracted and full forms

Most audio scripts include contracted forms such as *I've* or *He's* instead of the full forms *I have* and *he has*. It's such a standard feature of real speech and many written texts that it has to be incorporated. However, Speaker 2 illustrates a contrast of contracted forms and full forms that a scripted audio text is unlikely to include. Notice this part of the text where the speaker contrasts different restaurants:

> *There's the Greek place err just there, err there's the Italian over the road, there is the American style Atomic Burgers down there.*

He uses the contracted *there's* as he lists different restaurants but then uses the full form *there is* to refer to the American burger bar. This use of the full form indicates that the speaker thinks this place is especially good. It's a very subtle use of word stress in a sentence and one that many students would not notice so would not appear in many scripted audio texts.

Idiom, slang, jargon

Real speech tends to include more frequent instances of

local idiom, slang or jargon related to the speaker's background. Quite often this kind of language is cut in published materials because it dates and it's often very local or regional. Neither speaker uses the word *restaurant* but instead refer to *pizza places* or *the Greek place*. For a lower level student in another part of the world, this usage might well be confusing as it isn't a global term.

Pronunciation and accent

When recording real speech you cannot control the pronunciation features or accents of the speakers. In fact Speaker 1 has a strong Italian accent in the recording and Speaker 2 speaks in a southern English accent. Most coursebook recordings will tend towards neutral accents with standard British English (or equivalent in US publications) or other accents which are not too pronounced.

CONCLUSIONS ABOUT BALANCING REAL SPEECH AND GRADED SPEECH

Having identified the key features of real speech, a writer needs to decide how much these need to be added into a script which is being written for a certain level. Here are some tips for incorporating features of real speech:

- Contracted forms are a common part of everyday speech, so a lot of your scripts, especially dialogues and conversations will include them.

- If you decide to include features such as fillers, filled pauses and false starts to add authenticity, then write them into the script so that an actor knows where you want them to be added.

- As a general rule, don't include an error even though it is a feature of real speech; it's expected by teachers and students that a scripted text will demonstrate 'correct' English and including an error – unless it is clearly part of an error recognition exercise – will cause unnecessary confusion.

- As with errors, slang, jargon and idioms should only be included if they are part of the teaching aim, and usually only in scripts for higher level learners.

- If you need a particular feature of pronunciation to be added in (e.g. a certain stress), then make sure it's clearly indicated in the script. For example, underline a stressed word or indicate intonation by adding an arrow above a word or write [rising] or [falling] after the word or sentence.

- For accents, include notes on using particular accents in square brackets.

Task 7

Read this audio script for students of English for Academic Purposes at a B1/B2 level. The aim is to present the language needed for giving a presentation. Rewrite the script so it includes more features of real speech and sounds more authentic but without increasing the level of difficulty for students at this level.

Good morning everyone and thank you for coming. I am currently studying for my degree in Media Studies and so today I would like to present part of my dissertation on the subject of web-based media. Before I go into too much detail, I would like to give an overview of what we mean by

*web-based media for anyone who isn't familiar with this
aspect of media studies.*

*Basically, web-based media refers to anything on the
internet. So when we look at a website, we need to think
about the purpose of a website, analyse its target audience,
and think about the conventions that most websites follow.
To show you what I mean, take a look at this slide ...*

You can read a commentary on this task on page 78.

OTHER CONSIDERATIONS WHEN SCRIPTING AUDIO

Obviously, the linguistic purpose of the audio is uppermost
in your mind when writing a script – does it need to
illustrate a language point in context or is it being used to
develop a listening skill or aspect of pronunciation?
However, there are other factors to bear in mind when
scripting. But before reading about what those factors are,
try this task.

Task 8

Compare two drafts of a script prepared for a unit in an
Elementary coursebook on the topic of using technology in
the workplace. What are the key differences between them,
and why do you think the writer made the changes to draft
1?

Draft 1
A: Sorry, can you help?
B: Sure.
A: How do I use the new Intranet?
B: First of all, you need a password and remember to use
lower case letters. Don't use upper case letters. So when

33

you log in, here is *Company news*. And you can also send messages like this. First of all, click on *My intranet*. Next click on *Messages*. So it's similar to email. You have an inbox and you can send messages to people at work. OK?
A: That's great. Thanks.

Draft 2
Magda: Sorry. Can you help me?
Chen: Sure.
Magda: How do I use the new Intranet?
Chen: Do you have a password?
Magda: Yes, it's here. I'm trying to key it in, but it doesn't work.
Chen: That's because the password is in lower case letters. Don't use upper case letters.
Magda: Oh!
Chen: That's it. So here is *Company news*. And you can also send messages.
Magda: How?
Chen: First of all, click on *My intranet*. Next click on *Messages*. So it's similar to email. You have an inbox and you can send messages to people at work. OK?
Magda: That's great. Thanks.

You can read a commentary on this task on page 79.

Reproduced by permission of Oxford University Press. From *Business Result El*ementary *Student's Book* by David Grant, John Hughes and Rebecca Turner © Oxford University Press 2009

Adding context
It will help the listener's comprehension if he/she knows where a monologue or conversation is taking place. For example, if the conversation is happening at a conference,

then you could put that information in the rubric in the material; e.g. *Listen to the conversation at a conference and answer questions 1–6.* Alternatively, you could include a photograph showing people talking at a conference. However, it can also be helpful to make the context for the listening 'overt' by having a character say something like *The conference is busier than last year.* Or *Have you been to this conference before?* There's a danger that such sentences make the script less authentic but nevertheless it can help.

Sound effects

Another way to help with context and add some authenticity is to provide notes with the script on using sound effects. For example, if the conversation takes place in a railway station, the listening could begin with the background noise of a station announcement. Although ELT audios can't be too ambitious with background sound effects, most recording studios can add in effects such as background street noises, types of transport, doors closing, etc. For telephone calls, they can make the speaker sound as if he's talking down a phone. Indicate any sound effects using square brackets in your script.

Turn-taking and responding

When writing conversations between two or three people, as a general rule, keep each turn short. The danger of one person talking for a long time is that a listening student can lose track of what is being said. If the other characters often respond, ask clarifying questions or even echo something, it helps the listener to follow.

Numbers of speakers

Because it is for audio, having too many speakers will confuse the listener. Two people in a dialogue is ideal. Three people is manageable for a listener as long as the conversation uses names overtly to help distinguish between who is speaking. Four speakers becomes a real challenge and should be avoided in most cases. Any more speakers than that in one track[6] and you'll confuse teachers and students alike.

Gender

Other than the obvious reasons for having a fairly equal balance of male and female speakers in your scripts, one particular reason is so that the listener can easily distinguish who is speaking. For example, if you write a dialogue, using one man and one woman avoids any potential confusion. As soon as you increase the number of speakers then it becomes even more important to mix the genders; for example, with three speakers, one of them should be the opposite gender to help the listener follow who is speaking.

Naming the speakers

It's common in many scripts to see the speakers referred to as A, B and C, etc. Typically, this notation is used when the conversations are short or the purpose of the recording is a listen-and-repeat drill or a short pronunciation exercise. However, naming the speakers can be useful when a conversation is longer and especially when there are more than two speakers. With three speakers you often need to insert a name here and there to help students identify who is speaking. It's also useful for the design of a comprehension exercise because students can listen to what a particular person says and write it down.

---

[6] **track / track numbers**
A track is one recording on a CD or within an online file library. For example, a coursebook might come with around 60 tracks. Each of these will have a track number which appears in the book for ease of reference.

Accent

Using different accents is another way to make it clearer who is speaking but – more importantly – it reflects the use of English as a form of international communication and exposes students to a range of voices. In the past, the speakers in ELT scripts were often given the names of native speakers because the settings were often in the UK or USA. Nowadays however, scripts tend to reflect the fact that English is the lingua franca used between non-native speakers across national borders. So scripts might include someone with a French accent talking to someone else with a Japanese accent. As a result, you will also need to find names from different countries to use in your scripts. One way of doing this is to do an online search for lists of first names and surnames from different countries. Also make sure you check the gender of the names you are using; it isn't unheard for coursebooks to include a male speaker with a female name for example. Something a student from that country will gleefully point out to their teacher once the material is published! (See also the Resources And Further Reading section (page 74) at the end of this book for more sources of names for speakers.)

Note: In the chapter on writing video scripts (page 43), you will also find sections on developing narrative and characters, some of which are also relevant when writing audio scripts.

PREPARING THE FINISHED SCRIPT FOR A RECORDING STUDIO

If you are recording your audio scripts for use in your own lessons, then modern technology allows you to produce reasonable quality recordings at little cost. At a very basic level you can record voices with a smartphone. For something more professional – but still free – download the software *Audacity* (*sourceforge.net/projects/audacity/*)

which allows you to make and then edit a recording. With regard to the actors, you can probably ask colleagues, friends and family to read out the various parts.

However, if you are writing the script for a publisher, then the publisher will hire the services of a recording studio which specialises in producing audio for language learning materials. Although you will have very little direct contact with the studio until (possibly) the day of the recording it's useful to understand the process of preparing a script for the recording and how the recording sessions will work.

The producer of the recording will request a copy of the entire script in order to give a quote to the client/publisher. That quote will include the cost of hiring actors, the studio, a technician, editing time and facilities, and even the cost of delivering the copies of the recording. Once the price is agreed, the producer will go ahead and hire the actors and prepare for the recording. So at this stage the editor will need to make sure the script includes all of the following information:

- accents required (UK, US, French, Japanese, etc.)

- gender and approximate age of characters

- any particular personality or character types

- the location of a script which might require certain sound effects (e.g. background noise in the street)

- the level of the material and therefore how this affects the actors' speed of delivery and use of pauses

- notes on the main purpose of a track or how it will be used; for example, if it is being used to highlight an aspect of pronunciation then certain words might need to be in bold to help the actors get the desired result.

- notes on difficult or unusual pronunciation, e.g. for proper nouns or names.

The finalised script is the responsibility of the editor who will add in features such as narrator lines. These include rubrics if they are to be recorded before the main listening, track numbers and idents[7] (e.g. *A, B, C, Speaker 1, Speaker 2,* etc.) and any copyright information that has to go at the start or end of the complete recording.

Here is part of a listening script to accompany a business English coursebook which has been prepared for the recording studio. Notice the information that is included in addition to what the speakers will say:

Sample script for recording studio

[Track 32]

Narrator: *Unit 3, Track 12*

[One male and one female voice – Alex is early-50s and has a Spanish accent. Josey is from Canada and in her early-30s. They are meeting for the first time at a conference in Toronto. Sound of people talking in the background.]

Josey: *Hi! Are you Alex by any chance?*

---

[7] **idents**
In scripts, idents refer to the identities of the speakers. They might only be a letter such as 'A' or 'B' or 'Speaker 1' and 'Speaker 2', or they could be real names.

Alex: That's right. Pleased to meet you.

Josey: I'm Josey from Roxbo. We've spoken on the phone a few times.

Alex: Of course! Hi Josey. Nice to meet you at last!

THE DAY OF THE RECORDING

You may have the opportunity to attend the audio recording in person, along with the in-house editor. Alternatively, you may be invited to attend by Skype. Once the actors are hired and the studio is booked, everyone receives a call sheet[8] which gives details of time and place. On the actual day of the recording you will need to arrive at the studio in good time before the scheduled recording start time – this will give you an opportunity to meet the producer and the sound engineer and discuss any queries they have about the script, etc. You will also meet the actors as they arrive.

During the recording you will sit behind the producer with your editor. The actors will be working on the other side of the glass window in the studio. The producer is the person in charge and will lead the recording. After each track has been recorded he/she will ask for your opinion to check that it achieves what you wanted; this is especially true of pronunciation recordings where a specific result is required. All being well, for large parts of the recording, you won't need to comment. At this stage, everything should be evident from the script and it isn't the time for a writer to suddenly change a script. The cost of hiring a studio and the time involved doesn't allow for this, and any changes

---

[8] **call sheet**
This is the document sent out by the producer of the audio or video to the actors, listing when and where the recording or filming will take place, at what time and who is required to be there.

that do arise will be discussed with the editor before being implemented as they will possibly create knock-on effects for other elements of the material such as artwork, answer keys or associated exercises. A writer should only interrupt the recording proceedings if something is completely wrong; for example, if an actor is delivering the script in a way that won't work within the context of the exercise in the material.

HOW ACTORS WILL READ YOUR SCRIPT

When actors record materials for language learning, they are briefed to read only what is on the page. This means that you cannot assume they will add any features of real speech that are not written into the script. If you require a speaker to use a false start (e.g. *I mean, I mean, what I want to say is …*) then you need to write it in. This issue is especially important with regard to writing in any pronunciation features. If you expect a particular word to be stressed in a dialogue then you need to indicate that stress (perhaps by underlining it or even inserting a note to the actor in square brackets. (Square brackets [ ] are used in scripts for notes that aren't meant to be read aloud.) In a very few cases, some ad-libbing is allowed by actors but this is typically only done for advanced level material and you will need to make this clear in your scripting.

Once the recording session is over, it is left to the producer to edit the tracks and send them to the editor for checking; you might also receive a copy to listen to and check; note that re-recording of a track will only take place if there is something totally wrong such as an error in pronunciation recording. Otherwise, this is the final version and you won't hear it again until it's published.

That's the end of this section on writing scripts for audio recordings. As we have seen, it is a fine balancing act between writing a script which includes the target language at the right level and the authenticity of real speech. In addition, you have to bear in mind that audio doesn't allow for any visual context and the fact that there are limitations imposed by the realities of recording the script in a studio.

Now we will take the principles of script writing for audio and develop them for writing scripts for video materials.

3. How To Write Video Scripts

WHY VIDEO?

Task 9

Before you start reading this section, make a list of reasons why teachers use video in the classroom.

In the past, video used to be used to teach language but also to add fun to a lesson; it was notoriously used in lessons at the end of the week when it was thought students would enjoy a 'video lesson'. It's important to note that lots of students didn't necessarily have access to video at home, nor did they have videos in English so watching video in your English lesson did indeed have a novelty value. However, fast forward to the present day and any student with access to the internet has access to videos in English any time of the day. In addition, teachers with projectors or IWBs in their classroom can add in video to any lesson; in other words, the novelty factor has diminished.

You can watch the author of this book outlining typical uses of video in the classroom at *bit.ly/JH_YouTube* but in general there are the four main reasons that teachers use ELT video:

Language input
As with audio, students can listen to the spoken words in a video and use this as springboard into an area of grammar or vocabulary; for example, they could watch two people in a shop and learn expressions for shopping via the dialogue. However, since this is video, we could also show some of the different items in the shop on screen and use this as a way to introduce a variety of countable and uncountable nouns.

Skills
In many materials, video is used to develop (or test) students' listening skills. Many of the comprehension exercise types that accompany video resemble those used with audio. Of course its advantage over audio is that what's happening on screen makes the listening more accessible and students have a better chance at guessing meaning because they have a context or can see the people speaking.

Activating language
Video is also used in the classroom as a way to get students speaking or writing. For example, a teacher can start the lesson by playing a video with the sound off and students have to predict/imagine what the people in the video are saying. Alternatively, students are only played the soundtrack and don't see the screen; then they have to speculate about what is happening on screen.

Topics and content
For teachers who want to help students to understand a topic or new subject matter, then video can be very effective. For example, in business English teachers could show a class a documentary about a company or an interview with a CEO. In other words, we use videos in English to teach *about* something as well as teaching English.

Having seen how teachers are using video in the classroom, it's clearly important to know in what ways the teachers and students will use your videos. Diarmuid Carter of Digeo Productions specializes in ELT video. His advice for any ELT script writer starting out on a project is to 'know the function of the video. Some courses use the videos to kick-start debate. They want exciting videos, and they're often willing to sacrifice some vocabulary or grammar points to get them. For others the learning points are paramount, and while they will also want engaging videos, the language and grammar must take priority. The earlier you know how the video will be used, the better for the script.'

HOW IS WRITING FOR VIDEO DIFFERENT FROM WRITING FOR AUDIO?

Task 10

Think about using video instead of audio in the classroom. What does video offer that audio can't? How can it improve language learning?

You can read a commentary on this task on page 79.

The key difference between writing for video and audio is that you have to consider the visual elements and write those into the script. To some extent, we can transfer some of what we know from writing scripts for audio and apply that to writing for video. However, the danger with merely transferring an audio script onto video is that it's potentially quite dull; for example, if you take an audio script of two people ordering coffee in a café and turn it into video, then all you add is a view of a café and two actors at a table. In a way, you have gained little from the conversation taking place on audio.

One of the early rules taught to students at film school is to 'Show, don't tell'. In other words, if it can be shown on the screen visually, then don't script words to express it. Let's consider how this might be applied to an ELT video script. Imagine you want to teach the language for asking for and offering help. Your script might begin with something like this:

A: Can you help me move this box?
B: Sure. Where are we taking it?

But in a video, the script might read (and be laid out) like this:

We see an enormous cardboard box blocking the corridor in an office. Man A is struggling to lift it. Man B rushes up, looking at his watch. He tries to get round the box.

MAN A
Can you help?

MAN B
Sure.

They lift the box and move up the corridor to a doorway. Man A tries to turn into the doorway but the box is much too wide.

Task 11

Compare the two previous scripts. What does the video script offer the viewer that the audio script doesn't offer the listener?

You can read a commentary on this task on page 80.

You'll have noticed that the layout of the two scripts are different. This will be addressed in more detail later in this section.

Although the video in the previous example might be memorable because of the problems caused by a ridiculously large box, we also need to consider whether the students recall any of the language used if the main focus is visual. In other words, does the 'Show, don't tell' rule apply to ELT videos in the same way it does to movie making?

This issue faced me some years ago while working on a script for elementary students on checking in at a hotel. I wrote a dialogue between a visitor and a receptionist with useful phrases for checking in and dealing with some minor difficulties. I added notes on what the camera might show (e.g. hotel entrance, reception area, type of person behind the desk and so on).

The script was passed on to the director who went off to film it. The next time I was involved was for the final edit. The video started very much how I'd imagined it with some very nice outdoor establishing shots[9] of a taxi arriving at a hotel and the visitor stepping out and entering the hotel. What came as a surprise was the additional (and previously unscripted) voiceover narration which explained something to the effect of: *A visitor is arriving at the hotel to check in.* Why include this when the video already shows us?

When I questioned why this voiceover had been added to the script, the director argued that the 'Show, don't tell' rule doesn't always apply in ELT videos because the primary job of the video is to provide language input so sometimes it's necessary to add it in where you wouldn't normally include it; in other words, scripted ELT videos have a responsibility to 'Show AND tell'.

Whatever you think about the two views of video, I do think there's a balance to be struck between 'Show, don't

---

[9] **shot / establishing shot**
The shot is what the camera needs to film and what we see on screen. An *establishing shot* refers to the first shot in a film sequence which tells us where the action is taking place. For example, an establishing shot might show the outside of a hotel before we see another shot inside where the main action takes place.

tell' and 'Show and tell'. Certainly, for video which is being written in order to introduce key expressions, then there is a responsibility to include more overt language than you might normally. On the other hand, if the aim of the video is to stimulate interest or class discussion, something that's more visual with fewer words might be preferable. James Tomalin is a producer of ELT video with Oxford Digital Media and considers this balancing act: 'If your script includes a car broken down on the side of the road, then you have to ask yourself why a character needs to say *That car's broken down.* If the aim is to teach the verb *break down*, then you can justify it. Otherwise, why say it when we can see it?'

Task 12

As we have seen so far, in ELT videos we usually need to keep in mind the target language we want to teach. Nevertheless, the following exercise is a useful way to raise your awareness of how to script visually. It's a task that is often given to new students at film school. Read each phrase and consider how you might show it in a video without using any of the actual words. In particular, think about how you would use the context, character, gestures, location, etc. to achieve this.

1. I'm so angry, I could scream!
2. Sorry, can you repeat that? I didn't understand you.
3. I'll give you $10 for it.
4. Would you mind moving your car? It's in my space.
5. The bus is leaving. Run or we'll miss it!
6. I've never been to Paris before. It's wonderful!

You can read a commentary on this task on page 80.

4. Practical Points To Consider About Writing For Video

Writing visually is the obvious way in which writing for video is different to writing for audio, but if you are used to writing for audio, then there are some other key points to note when writing video scripts. They tend to be practical issues and all indirectly related to the budget. It's hard to overstress just what an impact the budget of filming has on what is possible. Unlike recording an audio, filming involves many more costs including one or more camera operators, a sound technician, the director/producer, actors, a place to film (studio or on location), props, costumes, and even transportation; as one video producer said to me: 'If you write that you want a helicopter in your video, then you need two helicopters because you need the other to film it from.'

So before you go off and write a script, you need to be aware of what limitations there may be on the video as a result of the budget. The following points should help you with this. Ideally, they are all points you will be made aware of in a brief from your publisher and – if they aren't – then ask about them. It will save a lot of time and heartache later on, if you do.

Location
When writing a script for audio, you can place it in any location you like. On the side of a Himalayan mountain with the wind rushing past or inside a helicopter flying across London. When writing a video script, your choice of location will affect the amount of time it takes to organise the filming and in turn, the cost. So a lot of the time you have to ask yourself why the dialogue has to be filmed in a particular place; for example, if your script says that a

conversation takes place between two people in a moving car, you have to ask yourself if it's crucial that the car is moving. Could they have the same conversation in a parked car because it will be much easier and therefore cheaper to film?

Mari Tudor Jones, who directs educational video, also points out that 'shooting on location is often less efficient because – for example – you're waiting for the noise of an overhead plane to pass or an interruption by a siren. Filming in a studio is easier and cheaper.' She also argues that 'filming against a white backdrop with creative use of props and objects can often achieve your purpose just as effectively as being in a real location'. In recent years many ELT videos, including the *New English File* videos (OUP), have used the white backdrop. Alternatively, you can shoot against a green screen in the studio which allows you to film actors and then insert images (still or moving) behind them afterwards.

Number of actors

Recording an audio script for a coursebook within the region of 100 different tracks requires lots of different voices. However, it can all be achieved with around six actors all playing different parts with different accents. In video this is not the case and new ELT video script writers often make the mistake of having too many characters. For example, if you are filming a hotel scene, you could include a business person arriving in a taxi, the taxi driver, the doorman, other guests in the lobby and a receptionist. To justify all these people you could give them all something to say. However, for such a short sequence it would be too expensive. In reality, the main target language needed for checking in at a hotel is that of the guest arriving and the receptionist. So while including all these extras might suit a

Hollywood blockbuster, you can't include them in an ELT video script.

Writing scripts for different levels

Another point to consider is that the publisher might be filming video materials to go with different levels of a course. So you are probably going to write a series of scripts used at elementary, pre-intermediate, intermediate and so on. If this is the case, then keep in mind that the same actors and locations can appear at different levels so try to write the different scripts in a way that they might reuse actors (or their characters) and the same locations.

Describe, don't tell

Writers who have moved from writing audio to video also have a tendency to overwrite their scripts according to script editors and directors. James Magrane of OUP's media department gives this advice: 'One thing worth remembering about writing for video is that you should "describe, don't direct". This means that in the narration sections of a drama script, for example, don't write that you want tracking shots or pans across vistas, just describe the vista. This is partly practical – you may not know the specifics of the location and what's possible – and partly politics – directors are by and large touchy folk who don't like to be told what to shoot.' His view is supported by the comment of another video director that inexperienced ELT writers have a tendency to 'overwrite when less is often more'.

5. Types Of Video Script

'Language teachers are using so much online video and so your scripts are competing with that.' Mari Tudor Jones (MTJ Media)

To spend an hour or so idly clicking through *YouTube* is to discover a vast range of different types of video. It's currently such an evolving form that it would be hard to define every type. In ELT, many teachers are now producing their own videos with their students writing scripts and performing them. Another trend in education video is to produce video content which teaches students something. Perhaps the best-known examples of this can be viewed at the Kahn Academy (*khanacademy.org*) which offers video lessons in 'maths, science, computer programming, history, art history, economics, and more'. Out of the idea that a student can watch the input for a subject at home has developed the 'flipped classroom'[10] approach where the input is delivered by video before the lesson so that lesson time is spent doing practice activities. The flipped classroom has an obvious attraction for English language teachers. It's easy to present a grammar point on the board and video it. Then students watch the presentation at home before the lesson so that during the lesson they can focus on using the new grammar in

---

[10] **flipped classroom**
The 'flipped classroom' refers to the idea of students studying formal input before the lesson and then using the lesson time to take part in more interactive tasks. In other words, instead of the teacher formally presenting some new language, students work on this at home, and then try out using it in the classroom with the teacher monitoring. This has become more realistic as an approach with the increasing use of technology; for example, a teacher can film him/herself presenting some grammar and students watch this at home. Then during the lesson, the teacher gives students freer practice exercises to do.

communicative activities. In fact you don't even need to record it yourself because there are countless teachers on *YouTube* who have already scripted and recorded their own language presentations, like this one: *youtube.com/watch?v=x8P6mp1dGk4.*

When it comes to writing video scripts for ELT publishers and a professional media company, writers are often required to script certain types of video and Diarmuid Carter (ELT video specialist at Digeo Productions) suggests that there are times when one is more appropriate than another: 'Short mini-dramas often suit beginners because you can contrive a situation to best suit what's in the book. Voiceover documentaries often suit profiles of things and places and presenter-led documentaries often suit abstract concepts that are difficult to illustrate visually but that a presenter can help to explain.'

As well as drama or documentaries, an increasing number of ELT videos are also making use of graphics and animation and so you will need to adjust your approach to the script according to the needs of the project. However, we can broadly categorise the type of ELT video scripts we write into two main categories: Dramas and Documentaries. So, the section that follows presents some examples of scripts written for these genres and how writers might develop their skills accordingly.

DRAMA SCRIPTS

The term 'drama' in ELT script writing has quite a broad meaning. At a basic level it is a fictional situation between fictional characters; for example, you might write a script in which two friends meet at a café and order coffee and a sandwich. It's a useful way to present the language in a visual and contextualised situation even if it's somewhat lacking in originality or what we might call 'real drama'. At a more sophisticated level, ELT video drama should also aim to present target language in a dramatic context with interesting characters and a strong narrative thread.

Not surprisingly then, writing drama scripts is probably the most challenging (and expensive) type of ELT script writing because to be successful it requires the balancing of three different skills:

- grading the language level and target key language.

- understanding the basic principles of how video scripts are written and constructed and how they are essentially different from an audio script.

- writing dramatic scripts with interesting characters and narratives.

The first skill of grading the language is the least challenging for us because we have presumably honed that skill after years of teaching and writing course materials and audio scripts. The second skill is something that can be acquired by working with experienced script editors and video producers (and of course by reading this book!). However, the third skill of writing real drama needs the skill of a TV script writer.

THE LAYOUT OF A DRAMA SCRIPT

Let's begin by considering how you might construct a basic script for a drama. Many ELT writers submit their scripts in the same way as an audio script with the speakers' lines and a few notes added about what's on the screen. Your publisher will be happy to accept your script in this way and then they will pass it on to a script editor who turns it into a finished document. This final script might follow certain conventions so that everyone involved in the process understands what will be filmed. Here is an extract from an ELT drama script that has been prepared for filming.

Task 13
Read the script and note the layout. How is it different from, for example, a script written for audio? Why do you think these conventions are used?

You can read a commentary on this task on page 81.

Episode 5

PART ONE

1. EXT. THE HOUSE – NIGHT

Establishing shot. The house is mysterious and dark. We see a flicker of torchlight inside.

2. INT. THE HOUSE: HENRY'S STUDY – NIGHT

Jenny and Luke are frantically searching through books on the bookshelf using torches. We see Jenny pulling out several books from the shelf.

JENNY
The Iliad, The Poems of Lord Byron,
The Complete Works of Shakespeare ...
nothing about an old man!

We see Luke doing the same.

LUKE
Not even a picture on the front cover.

JENNY
(pointing torch to paintings)
What about those paintings?
Anything there?

LUKE
I've already checked them. Nothing.

Luke turns around to the bookshelf.

LUKE
Should we look through each book?

JENNY
That could take forever and we don't have time.
(frustrated) Oh, this is hopeless.

Jenny's mobile rings. Jenny and Luke suddenly freeze. She checks the caller ID.

Reproduced by permission of Oxford University Press. From *English File Intermediate Plus Student's Book* by Christina Latham-Koenig, Clive Oxenden and Mike Boyle © Oxford University Press 2014

DEVELOPING DIALOGUE, CHARACTERS AND NARRATIVE

As mentioned previously, developing the third skill of writing intrinsically interesting drama is probably the toughest challenge for most of us. As Mari Tudor Jones remarks on some of the scripts she works with: 'ELT writers are naturally good at writing drama at the right language level, but what's lacking is character and narrative.'

It is not within the size and scope of this book to provide a whole course in developing the skills of narrative and character. There are in fact many more books available which can help you to do this and some are recommended in the Resources And Further Reading section (page 74) at the end of this book. However, it is worth looking at a few quick techniques that can be applied to your scripts in order to develop characters and narrative.

In the previous section on writing scripts for audio recordings, we looked at the balance between writing dialogue for the students' level and writing dialogue which feels authentic and includes features of real speech. However, it's worth noting that good drama doesn't necessarily rely on authentic dialogues but instead the writer needs to concentrate on what makes good dialogue.

In an article on how to write good dialogue for ELT materials, the ELT author Nicola Prentis comments: 'Aiming for authentic dialogue is impossible. What a writer should be focussing on is good dialogue. By that I mean dialogue that's entertaining enough to want to listen to for its own sake and not purely for the purpose of learning how to say something. Students have heard Hans the Wooden Businessman check into Hotel Anonymous and enquire when breakfast is a million times. Just because they're in a classroom shouldn't mean we sacrifice some kind of entertainment value. For that, taking tips from screen and fiction writers is the key to success.'

Prentis, N. *Writing good dialogue for audio and video* (Jan 2015) Modern English Teacher Volume 42, Issue 1

The key starting point for 'good dialogue', according to Prentis is 'strong characters'. In her article she suggests a variety of ways to develop your characters such as cutting out a collection of photographs of interesting-looking people from magazines. Then choose two and imagine them having the kind of dialogue you need to write for your video (or audio). How will their gender, age, race, clothing style, etc., affect the way the lines are spoken?

Video producer Mari Tudor Jones endorses this view that ELT scripts need developed characters. Partly because it naturally aids the dialogue but also because it helps the actors who have to deliver the lines to the camera: 'It's much harder for an actor to act if there's no character. In that situation, it's just words and language but an actor naturally wants to do something with it.' She suggests that ELT writers try adding more detail about characters in their scripts; so instead of a line like *Man in shop – middle aged,* try expanding the detail so the actor can bring it to life.

Imagine you have to write a dialogue between two people meeting in a café. How can you develop the characters? One way is to create a backstory[11] for both people by asking questions about them, for example:

- Who are they?

- Why are they meeting each other?

- Have they met before?

- Do they often meet at this particular café? Why? Why not?

- What were they doing five minutes before this scene?

- What does one of the characters want to get out of the meeting?

---

[11] **backstory**
A term referring to the story behind a character in a story; writers will develop backstories for characters in order to develop their personalities and to make them seem more real.

The novelist Kurt Vonnegut also believed that character was central to all good stories and that the main character always wanted to get something by the end of the narrative. So, a useful technique when writing your script is to consider want the main character wants by the end. Of course, if the setting is a café or a hotel, then the main character may only want to buy a coffee or to check in to a comfortable room. If that's the case, then one way to add narrative to a mundane situation is to introduce problems and obstacles for the main character which prevent him/her from getting what he/she wants.

To understand how introducing problems can add narrative to an ELT script, compare two versions of the same script. In version 1, a hotel guest checks in with no problems. In version 2, things go wrong.

Version 1

RECEPTIONIST
Hello, can I help you?

GUEST
I have a reservation. My name is Long. Jane Long.

RECEPTIONIST
Ah, yes. For two nights.

GUEST
That's right.

RECEPTIONIST
Can I have your passport and a credit card?

GUEST
Sure. Here you are.

RECEPTIONIST
Can you fill in this form?

GUEST
Of course.

RECEPTIONIST
Here is your key. Your room is 301 on the 3rd floor.
Breakfast is between 7 and 10 on the first floor.

GUEST
Thank you very much.

Version 2

RECEPTIONIST
(unsmiling) Hello?

GUEST
I have a reservation for two nights. My name's Bond.
Jane Bond.

Receptionist types into computer.

RECEPTIONIST
Sorry, you're not here. I have a reservation for James
Bond.

GUEST
I think that's a mistake. It happens a lot.

RECEPTIONIST
(suspicious) Really? Can I have a credit card and your
passport, please?

GUEST
Sure. Here you are ...

Receptionist swipes card.

RECEPTIONIST
Sorry but the machine won't accept it.

GUEST
I don't understand. Can you try again?

RECEPTIONIST
And also this isn't your passport ...

As you can see, there's nothing wrong with the dialogue in version 1 and it gives students the target language they need. But in dramatic terms, version 2 is more interesting. By creating conflict and therefore tension, the two characters also become more interesting. Arguably, your students need to be prepared with the ordinary formulaic language in version 1 but sometimes they might need to deal with problematic situations so version 2 also offers a useful (as well as a more engaging) context. Note that the technique of introducing difficulties for main characters is tried and tested, especially in comedy. Watch some classic visual comedy such as *Mr Bean* and *Fawlty Towers* which are based around the main character trying (with or without eventual success) to get/do something.

As I said at the beginning of this short section on character and narrative, you can discover more ideas for developing your characters and narrative by looking at the Resources And Further Reading section (page 74) which lists some useful titles. Perhaps the combination of what I've suggested above and the ideas of others can help to inject some drama that is sometimes lacking in ELT videos.

DOCUMENTARIES

As mentioned earlier in this book, the use of documentaries in ELT materials has become very popular in recent years. It reflects the popularity of similar videos on *YouTube* as well as a modern fascination with watching reality. Another attraction for ELT publishers must also be the relative cheapness in producing documentaries in comparison to producing drama.

As far as the materials writer is concerned, your role in the process of creating a documentary script will feel very different to writing drama and will depend upon the nature of the project. In many ways, writing documentary scripts won't feel as much of a challenge as writing drama because you are writing about something real. You will also apply similar skills to those you use when selecting interesting texts and topics for coursebook writing. You want a subject that is intrinsically interesting and that offers students the opportunity to learn certain target language; the key mantra is that 'students should learn ABOUT something as well as learning English'.

The style and format of a documentary can vary. On screen there is a range of ways subjects can be illustrated, including:

- filming original footage of the subject

- using existing footage which can be edited

- using an existing documentary but replacing the narration so the language is graded

- interviewing an expert on the subject

- interviewing people in the street

- using photographs and images with narration

- creating graphics and animation which are added to live action documentary or used instead of live action (sometimes referred to as kinetic typography videos – you can see an example here: *youtube.com/watch?v=4B2xOvKFFz4*).

In the rest of this section I'm going to outline the way in which three documentaries were written and developed for ELT courses. This will illustrate some of the different approaches that can be taken when scripting video documentaries.

DOCUMENTARY 1: THE CITY OF SANTIAGO

Approach: filming and editing footage with narration
The aim of this OUP video for *International Express* was to introduce the city of Santiago and the language students need for describing a city. Footage of the city was filmed specially for the video though sometimes publishers will use so-called 'stock footage', film that already exists and is purchased and edited in. (Another way of achieving a similar documentary effect for less money would be to use still photographs combined with narration.)

As a basic layout, the script is written in two columns with the narration on one side and notes about what we can see on the other. (Note that the abbreviation *GV* means 'general views'.) You can watch the finished video here: *youtube.com/watch?v=JZQUYsZhPn4*.

Reproduced by permission of Oxford University Press. From *International Express Elementary Student's Book* by Angela Buckingham, Alastair Lane and Bryan Stephens © Oxford University Press 2014

Voiceover	Images
Santiago is the capital of Chile.	GVs Santiago
It's a large, busy city in a beautiful location.	View of mountains from Santiago
To the east of the city are the Andes, the longest mountain range in the world.	The Andes from Santiago
To the west , there's the Chilean Coastal Range. It's shorter than the Andes, and the Andes are more famous, but the Chilean Coastal Range is just as beautiful.	The Chilean Coastal Range from Santiago
An hour away is the Pacific Ocean, the largest ocean in the world.	The Pacific
Almost five and a half million people live in Santiago.	People in Santiago
It's by far the largest city in Chile, but it's not the biggest in South America. It's smaller than São Paulo, Bogotá, Lima, Rio de Janeiro and Caracas.	GVs Santiago
But Santiago is still one of the most exciting cities in South America.	GVs
Santiago combines the modern with the traditional.	Modern buildings in Santiago Old building in Santiago
This is the city centre. It's the busiest area of the city and the buildings here are taller and more modern than the buildings in Santiago's older areas.	Santiago city centre
But there are lots of beautiful, historical buildings here too.	Classical architecture
This is La Moneda Palace. The Chilean president lives here, and it's one of the most popular tourist attractions in the city.	La Moneda Palace
The San Francisco church is the oldest building in the city. In fact, it's almost as old as the city itself.	San Francisco church
It has a bell tower and an old clock.	Bell tower and clock
As well as the interesting old buildings, Santiago also has beautiful scenery.	GVs
The mountains in the distance are pretty to look at, and they're home to some of the best adventure centres in Latin America.	Sports in Santiago
Inside or outside, there's always something to do in Santiago.	GVs
It is one of the most exciting cities in South America and lies in one of the most beautiful areas of the world.	Panoramic view of Santiago

DOCUMENTARY 2: WOMEN IN SPACE

Approach: using an existing documentary and rewriting the narration

Unlike the previous documentary about Santiago, this documentary about the first ever female US astronauts reuses existing video footage and so there was no need to film new material or do any editing. Instead, the writer watched the original documentary and wrote a narration which was recorded and added to the film. This replaced the existing narration which was inappropriate for the target students in terms of level.

Task 14

The script below shows the timings for the film in the first column. The second column contains the original narration from the documentary and the writer's new version is in the final column. You can watch the video with the original narration here: *bit.ly/Women_In_Space*.

Compare the two scripts and think about how and why the writer adapted the narration for elementary level students.

You can read a commentary for this task on page 81.

Timing	Original narration	Narration for Elementary level*
00.00– 00.18	Since the US space program began in 1958, NASA has achieved much in the realm of space exploration. From lunar landings to voyages into the depths of our solar system, NASA has built a storied history.	NASA began in 1958. It put a man on the Moon in 1969. Spacecraft like Voyager 1 and 2 discovered new places in our solar system and the space shuttle flew into space and back again.
00.19– 00.50	In the early days, space was a man's world. All that changed on June 18, 1983 when Sally Ride became the first American	In the early days of NASA, space was a man's world. But on the 18 June 1983, Sally Ride was the first

	woman to rocket toward the heavens aboard the space shuttle Challenger. A doctor of Physics, she was recruited by NASA as one of six female astronaut candidates for the shuttle program. While her first job was as a mission control communicator to orbiting shuttles, Sally Ride soon found herself in orbit during 1983's STS7 mission.	American woman in space. Sally was a doctor of Physics and she was part of a group of six candidates to be the first female astronaut. Sally soon got the job and went into space on the Challenger space shuttle.
00.51–01.28	And although the Russian space program had sent women into space as early as 1963, Ride's journey into space was a first ever for the U.S. Aboard the shuttle Challenger she served as a mission specialist, helping deploy two satellites and perform scientific experiments over six days. Shortly after her return, Ride reflected on what her journey into space meant. (Ride speaking:) "I was asked at a press conference just before our flight what I thought about being the first US woman astronaut. I was quoted as saying that it was no big deal."	The Russians sent the first women into space in 1963, but Sally Ride was the first for the USA. She helped to launch two satellites and did scientific experiments over six days. After she returned from the journey, Sally gave talks across the USA.
01.29–01.58	"What the astronaut meant to say was that technically as far as NASA's concerned it was no big deal. On another level, the United States sending a woman into space was a very important event for at least 53% of the population and I'm very proud of that." Sally Ride would venture into space once more, in 1984. And since that time others have become trailblazers as well.	In particular, her journey was important for women and many travelled to listen to her. Sally went into space one more time – in 1984. And after her, there were other women astronauts and other 'firsts'.
01.59–02.32	Physician-turned-astronaut Mae Jemison became the first African-American woman in space during shuttle Endeavour's 1992 mission. During orbit she performed experiments involving	Mae Jemison was a physician and became the first African-American woman in space with the space shuttle Endeavour in 1992. Then, in 1995,

	life sciences, materials sciences and bone cell research. In 1990, astronaut Eileen Collins became the first female shuttle pilot aboard Discovery. Collins commanded two space shuttle missions including the important return to flight mission in July 2005, the first after the 2003 Colombia disaster.	Eileen Collins became the first female pilot, with the space shuttle Discovery. And she flew two more times in 1999 and 2005.
02.33– end	Since Sally Ride's momentous flight into space, the ranks of female astronauts have grown. And in a male dominated field they hold a special position as role models for young women everywhere who dream of reaching the stars.	So as a result of Sally Ride, and many more female astronauts after her, young women – as well as young men – now dream of becoming astronauts and a journey into space.

From *Life Elementary*, National Geographic Learning

DOCUMENTARY 3: MEMORY AND LANGUAGE LEARNING

Approach: vox pops and animation graphics
Many ELT videos, and especially the documentaries, include interviews with real people. These are either short interviews interspersed with related footage, or the entire video is made of up of short interviews. These interviews are sometimes with an expert or they are sometimes ordinary people in the street expressing an opinion; these types of interviews are often called 'vox pops' from the Latin *vox populi* which means 'voice of the people'.

The advantage of the vox pop format over the longer interview is that they are short, require less specialist content knowledge on the part of the student, and the kinds of responses given will often reflect those of the students themselves so the vox pops have intrinsic interest and model the type of language a student might use. The role of the writer is to script questions that will elicit useful answers; this writing combines your ability to grade the language level of a question with the skills of a journalist to formulate effective questions. You may also be called upon to brief the people being interviewed.

In the following example I wrote three questions for a short video about learning languages. We interviewed four people who had experience of learning another language 'off the street' in a studio. They were briefed on the questions in advance but the responses were their own. In every case we filmed them at least twice and in between takes we made suggestions on how they might make their responses clearer given that the materials were for students at around a low A2 level. Here is part of a transcript of the final version:

> *Question: When you hear or see a new word in the language, how do you memorise it?*

01.36–01.47 [Spanish speaker talking about learning English] I've got a book and every time I learn a new word I write it down and I also write the definition so I can go back to it and memorise it.

01.48–02.03 [English speaker talking about learning French] I use different techniques. I might think: 'Does it sound like something I know? Does it look like something I know?' For example, un plat is 'a plate' and I think: 'It's like a plate but without the e.'

Extracts from *Life Elementary* Unit 10 Video, National Geographic Learning

Whilst the vox pops speakers gave useful, clear answers, as it stands the above script would work nearly as well if played on audio. However, we filmed the speakers against a green screen in a studio which allows any kind of graphic image to be placed behind the speaker after the filming has been done. This is a relatively quick, cheap and straightforward way to add visual impact and interest to a video. For example, for a drama you could film two actors against a green screen and then put a picture of the Eiffel Tower behind them in order to suggest the dialogue is taking place in Paris. In the case of these vox pops we wanted to add visual interest by adding small animation sequences next to the speaker. So, after the initial scripting of the questions, the next stage was to script instructions for animation to be added.

Here is the same part of the video above but this time the script includes notes on the animation and graphics which were then added at the editing stage afterwards.

Vox pops script	Animation and graphics to be added
When you hear or see a new word in the language, how do you memorise it?	Put spoken question on the screen with background music.
01.36–01.47 I've' got a book and every time I learn a new word I write it down and I also write the definition so I can go back to it and memorise it.	We see a pen and notebook to the left of the speaker. The pen starts writing.
01.48–02.03 I use different techniques. I might think: "Does it sound like something I know? Does it look like something I know? For example, *un plat* is 'a plate' and I think: 'It's like *a plate* but without the *e*.'"	Draw a plate, a fork and a knife to the right of the speaker. The word *plate* appears above it. The letter *e* drops off the end of the word *plate*.

Extracts from *Life Elementary* Video 'Memory and Language Learning', National Geographic Learning

6. Final Checklist

That nearly brings you to the end of this book. To sum up the main content, here is a checklist of 20 questions to consider when writing an ELT script. Clearly, not every question will be relevant to every type of script since, as we have seen, this will depend upon whether you are writing for audio or video, listening skills or speaking skills, documentary or drama, and whatever other types of scripts are set to emerge in the future. However, it will be useful to refer to this list from time to time and remind yourself of the key points.

1   Do you know the purpose of your script?

2   What level is the script for?

3   Will the script need to include certain target language?

4   How much will you grade the language to the level?

5   Can you include features of real speech and make it sound authentic?

6   Is the context clear from the script?

7   Are you going to include any sound effects or music?

8   Is there the right number of speakers without it becoming confusing for the listener?

9   Is there a good range of genders, names, nationalities and accents?

10   Does it need pronunciation for any words, expressions or sentences?

11 For a video script, how much emphasis will be on the visual elements? (e.g. 'show, don't tell' or 'show and tell')

12 Are the choices of locations realistic in terms of practicalities and budget?

13 Have you described your locations clearly but not to the extent of telling the director how to film them?

14 Is the number of characters in your video script realistic and/or necessary in terms of budget?

15 How interesting are the characters in your video script and will an actor know how to play them?

16 Can you improve the storyline or narrative in any way?

17 For a documentary, will you make use of photographs, footage or any other types of graphics or animations?

18 Will the documentary make use of existing footage or will new footage need to be filmed?

19 If the video includes interviews with real people, have you prepared the questions which will encourage useable responses?

20 Have you laid out and formatted your final draft of the script (audio or video) clearly so that an editor and producer can easily work with it?

Task 15

In Task 1 (page 9) at the very beginning of this book you were asked to consider the types of skills that someone writing ELT scripts might require. Look back at your notes and reflect on what you have read and learnt since. Have any of your views changed with regard to the importance of certain skills? Are there any skills that you would add to your original list? Which areas of ELT scriptwriting do you think you will need to develop further in the future?

Resources And Further Reading

WRITING SCRIPTS

Kenyon, S. (2010) *The Writer's Digest Character Naming Sourcebook Writer's Digest Books*
This book contains over 25,000 first names and surnames for more than 45 countries. It was written for novelists and authors but is useful when you need a name for a speaker from a specific country or region of the world. One word of warning is that it includes historical and legendary names which will sound dated nowadays, so you'll need to cross-check.

Field, S. (2005) *Screenplay* Delta
Syd Field's book is considered the bible of screenplay writing by the Hollywood film industry and is used film schools. Chapter 13 is about the form of a screenplay with details on conventions for formatting your video scripts. The book is aimed at writing a full-length film but you will also find ideas on developing areas such as character and narrative.

ONLINE SOFTWARE FOR FORMATTING SCREENPLAYS

Celtx (*celtx.com*) and Final Draft (*finaldraft.com*) offer online and downloadable tools for formatting screenplays.

This download (*http://downloads.bbc.co.uk/ writersroom/scripts/screenplaytv.pdf*) is a style guide to writing video scripts. It is published by the BBC but the guidelines can also be followed for writing scripts for ELT video. For more examples of different formats for scriptwriting also see the BBC's Writer's Room (*bbc.co.uk/writersroom/writers-lab/medium-and-format*).

ELT AUTHORS MENTIONED IN THIS BOOK

Peter Viney
When publishers eventually stopped selling his video titles
from the 80s and 90s, Peter Viney started distributing them
himself via his website (*viney.uk.com*)and they continue to
be used in classrooms around the world. In addition to this,
Peter has a blog (*peterviney.wordpress.com*) with a section
of articles on ELT and ELT videos. Although some of the
references in the articles feel dated in places, many of ideas
and comments are still very relevant and of interest and use
to writers of video material.

Vicki Hollett
The well-known ELT author Vicki Hollett began writing
video scripts for publishers but now produces her own
independently made videos at *Simple English Videos*
(*simpleenglishvideos.com*) and she also writes about video
in ELT on her blog (*vickihollett.com*).

Ben Goldstein
Ben has written various articles and books about using
images in ELT. His website also includes articles about
video (*bengoldstein.es/?s=video*).

ELT AUDIO AND VIDEO PRODUCTION COMPANIES WHO
CONTRIBUTED TO THE RESEARCH IN THIS BOOK

MTJ Media: *mtjmedia.com*
Oxford Digital Media: *oxforddigitalmedia.co.uk*
Cambridge Media Solutions:
cambridgemediasolutions.com
Tom Dick & Debbie Video Production:
tomdickanddebbie.co.uk
Digeo Productions: *digeoproductions.com*

Commentaries On Tasks

TASK 4

Audio script 1

This text type falls into the category of 'talk' or 'documentary'. In the book, students could look at the photographs taken by Nick Veasey and then listen to how they were taken. It's an example of an information-rich text type which is often used to develop listening skills in some way. Students will probably listen once for gist and then listen again for more detail. This kind of script also lends itself to teaching items of vocabulary or grammar. For example, in this case, the text is full of references to ways of working and includes some useful vocabulary that could be focused on in accompanying exercises.

Audio script 2

This is typical of dialogues which have been written to model useful expressions in a real transactional situation. This kind of script normally has exercises in the student's book which focus on students listening for and identifying the key phrases and the functional purpose. Then they do a roleplay activity in which they recreate a similar dialogue.

Audio script 3

This script is written for pronunciation practice. Students listen to each phrase and try to reproduce it. In the actual recording, the emphasis is on the intonation rising on the first noun and falling on the second noun. (The script writer would have supplied notes on the rise-fall patterns in the original draft so it could be recorded correctly.)

Audio script 4

This script uses the format of a journalist interviewing someone. This kind of interview format is a favoured vehicle in many ELT materials because it's a useful way to introduce a particular language point. In this example, the script is clearly aimed at demonstrating how the present perfect is used in question forms and the tense is also contrasted with the past simple. While this overuse of a language point makes the script sound inauthentic, it does nevertheless provide a contextualized way to present the grammar.

TASK 5

Here are some possible text types for items 2–6:

2. The first and second conditional
These two grammar structures are often presented in the context of a negotiation between two people because this type of conversation often requires the use of conditionals (e.g. *If I offer you $50, will you sell it?*)

3. A lexical set of film genres (e.g. *sci-fi, romantic comedy*, etc.)
A radio programme about the latest film releases would include this lexical set.

4. Collocations with the verbs *make* and *do*
These collocates could occur in a range of text types, however, someone describing or being interviewed about everyday routines or what they do in the workplace would guarantee the use of *make* and *do*.

5. The pronunciation feature of contrastive stress
To present the use of contrastive stress in an authentic situation requires a context in which someone needs to check information; e.g. *Did you say thirty or thirteen?* For this reason, it is often presented in the context of a

telephone call with the caller asking for and writing down information.

6. Useful phrases for asking for directions
The obvious context here is to have a tourist lost in a city and asking a passer-by for directions. Alternatively, it could be a message left on a person's voicemail giving directions to a house.

TASK 7

Here is an example of how you might include more elements of real speech in the rewritten script. Note that the key language and structure remains the same but with minimum changes it feels a little more authentic. Also, making the speaker from a distinct region or country and adding notes on the accent to be used all add to the script's sense of authenticity.

[Middle East accent]
Mujahid: Err, OK. Good morning everyone. Thanks for coming. I'm currently studying for my degree in Media Studies and so today I'd like to present part of my dissertation on the subject of web-based media. OK? Now, before I go into too much detail, I'd like to give an overview of what we mean by web-based media. You know, for anyone who isn't familiar with this aspect of media studies.

Err, basically, web-based media refers to anything on the internet. So, erm, when we look at a website, we need to think about the purpose of a website, analyse its target audience, and we need to think, err ... to think about the conventions that most websites follow. Right. To show you what I mean, take a look at this, err, [clicks on slide] slide ...

TASK 8

First of all, notice that in both scripts the first three lines of the dialogue remain unchanged because we are establishing the context for the conversation and the relationship between the speakers. However, in draft 1, Chen goes on to give a monologue about how to use the new company intranet. If the script was for video, the visual elements would make this easier to follow. However, for an audio recording, his monologue would be hard to follow in isolation. Instead, draft 2 is much more conversational with Magda and Chen turn-taking. Although dialogues of this kind can have a feeling of inauthenticity, within the limitations of audio and the level of the target student, this is often necessary. In draft 2 the speakers are given names, which helps to add a sense of context.

TASK 10

ELT author Peter Viney talks about what video brings to a classroom that audio can't:

'When I can see people, when I can see visual signals, when I can see contexts, I can see facial expression, everything becomes clear … . You know if people are joking, if they are serious, angry, gestures, stance, movement, all this information comes with video. With video you are taking the blindfold off.'

Watch Vicki Hollett's interview with Peter Viney here: *youtube.com/watch?v=JMBpDmH8W2s*.

TASK 11

As you can see from the video script, the speakers' words can be briefer because we infer so much more meaning from the visual elements. It's also noticeable how much more we can add with video in a short space of time in terms of content, characters, plot and humour; within 30 seconds of video we discover the box is comically enormous, we are in a workplace, one person is really struggling, the other person is in a hurry but has to help because the box is blocking his way.

TASK 12

Here are some suggested ways to replace the spoken words with something visual:

1. I'm so angry, I could scream! – A close up on an actor's face looking angry at a situation.

2. Sorry, can you repeat that? I didn't understand you. – A quizzical look from one person to another.

3. I'll give you $10. – Holding out $10 and gesturing towards the object for sale.

4. Would you mind moving your car? It's in my space. – Pointing a finger at the car and then pointing in the opposite direction.

5. The bus is leaving. Run or we'll miss it! – A bus pulling off from the bus stop and two people running to catch it.

6. I've never been to Paris before. It's wonderful! – A person looking up in awe at the Eiffel Tower.

TASK 13

Unlike an audio script, the layout for a drama script makes it very clear for everyone involved to see what is happening on screen and what is being said. Note that locations are given in capitals with some abbreviations like INT. and EXT. (interior shot and exterior shot). The action sequences are described in sentences going across the whole page. Character names (in capitals) are in the centre of the page with spoken words centred beneath, so as not to be confused with on-screen description. For a more detailed description of the conventions for the format of a written screenplay including details such as visual effects, etc., refer to the Resources And Further Reading section (page 74). Remember that when you work with a publisher and video producer, they will also advise you on layout or edit the script themselves to fit the exact format required.

TASK 14

In order to write a narration that can be used with Elementary level students, the writer has:

- kept the key facts (names, places, dates, etc.) from the original where possible

- simplified the sentence structure

- removed low frequency vocabulary and expressions (e.g. *the realm of space exploration*)

- increased the number of higher frequency words

- made the target language more overt; in this case the video was used to recycle the past simple tense from an earlier grammar presentation in the book.

Glossary

Audiolingualism (also Audiolingual Method)
Audiolingualism was based on the belief that language learning was about habit formation. Learners listened to and repeated dialogues in the form of a drill. As recording technology developed, the idea of classrooms as language laboratories emerged with rows of learners wearing headphones and the teacher controlling what each student was listening to.

authenticity
In recent years, ELT materials have put an emphasis on the use of authentic texts in the classroom. For example, using articles from real newspapers or recordings from TV documentaries. In contrast, coursebooks have been criticised for their inauthenticity with their gapfill exercises and drills. Nowadays, most teachers and writers assume that a mixture of authenticity and inauthenticity is desirable. As a result, many published texts and scripts tend to be 'realistic' rather than '100% authentic'.

backstory
A term referring to the story behind a character in a story; writers will develop backstories for characters in order to develop their personalities and to make them seem more real.

call sheet
This is the document sent out by the producer of the audio or video to the actors, listing when and where the recording or filming will take place, at what time and who is required to be there.

Direct Method / Natural Method
The Direct and Natural Methods were two approaches that

emerged in the late 19th century in reaction to **Grammar Translation**. They emphasised use of the first language only in order to reflect the way a first language is learned 'naturally'. Learners were exposed to the spoken form before the written form, so teachers often followed scripted dialogues with students.

functional-situational

This refers to the approach in a syllabus or materials to present language as functions and/or in a situation. For example, you might have the function of 'asking for information about a product' and the situation is 'at the shop'. This way of organising language is typically used in tourist phrasebooks and materials that help learners prepare for using English in specific contexts (e.g. travelling abroad).

flipped classroom

The 'flipped classroom' refers to the idea of students studying formal input before the lesson and then using the lesson time to take part in more interactive tasks. In other words, instead of the teacher formally presenting some new language, students work on this at home, and then try out using it in the classroom with the teacher monitoring. This has become more realistic as an approach with the increasing use of technology; for example, a teacher can film him/herself presenting some grammar and students watch this at home. Then during the lesson, the teacher gives students freer practice exercises to do.

Grammar Translation

A method of teaching based on the way in which Latin was once taught. Grammar is regarded as being at the centre of language teaching and is formally presented to the students and then tested by having students translate sentences either into their own language or from their own language into

English. This method of teaching was highly influential on the language classroom into the early and middle part of the 20th century.

idents

In scripts, idents refer to the identities of the speakers. They might only be a letter such as 'A' or 'B' or 'Speaker 1' and 'Speaker 2', or they could be real names.

shot / establishing shot

The shot is what the camera needs to film and what we see on screen. An establishing shot refers to the first shot in a film sequence which tells us where the action is taking place. For example, an establishing shot might show the outside of a hotel before we see another shot inside where the main action takes place.

track / track numbers

A track is one recording on a CD or within an online file library. For example, a coursebook might come with around 60 tracks. Each of these will have a track number which appears in the book for ease of reference.

Titles in this series are ...

A Lexicon For ELT Professionals
How ELT Publishing Works
How To Plan A Book
How To Write And Deliver Talks
How To Write Audio and Video Scripts ↗
How To Write Business English Materials †
How To Write CLIL Materials
How To Write Corporate Training Materials †
How To Write Critical Thinking Activities ↗
How To Write EAP Materials †
How To Write ESOL Materials †
How To Write ESP Materials †
How To Write Exam Preparation Materials
How To Write Film And Video Activities
How To Write For Digital Media
How To Write Graded Readers
How To Write Grammar Presentations And Practice
How To Write Inclusive Materials
How To Write Primary Materials
How To Write Pronunciation Activities
How To Write Reading And Listening Activities ↗
How To Write Secondary Materials
How To Write Speaking Activities ↗
How To Write Teacher's Books
How To Write Vocabulary Presentations And Practice ↗
How To Write Worksheets
How To Write Writing Activities ↗

Our paperback compendiums

↗ *How To Write Excellent ELT Materials: The Skills Series*
This book contains the six titles marked ↗ above.

† *How To Write Excellent ELT Materials: The ESP Series*
This book contains the five titles marked † above.

For further information, see **eltteacher2writer.co.uk**

Printed in Great Britain
by Amazon